The Industrial Revolution

Debra J. Housel, M.S.Ed.

Publishing Credits

Historical Consultant
Fernando A. Pérez, M.A.Ed.

Editors
Wendy Conklin, M.A.
Torrey Maloof

Editorial Director
Emily R. Smith, M.A.Ed.

Editor-in-Chief
Sharon Coan, M.S.Ed.

Creative Director
Lee Aucoin

Illustration Manager
Timothy J. Bradley

Publisher
Rachelle Cracchiolo, M.S.Ed.

Teacher Created Materials
5301 Oceanus Drive
Huntington Beach, CA 92649-1030
http://www.tcmpub.com
ISBN 978-0-7439-0660-9

Printed by: 51497
Printed in: Taiwan

Table of Contents

The Birth of the Industrial Revolution

In the 1700s, a great **revolution** (rev-uh-LOO-shuhn) began in Great Britain. It was a revolution of industry. It marked the end of people living in rural societies and making the things they needed by hand. People began creating machines to do the hard work. Factories were built and banks were opened. This time is known as the Industrial (in-DUHZ-tree-uhl) Revolution, and it changed the history of the world forever.

Why did it start in Great Britain? Only this nation had all the necessary factors. It had wealth and men who were willing to risk their money. It had a banking system to pair savers' funds with investors. It also had raw materials such as coal and iron.

Great Britain was the first country to have cotton mills.

The Industrial Revolution started in Great Britain. It did not take long for the changes to reach the United States.

Also, in Great Britain there were more people than were needed to work on the farms. This offered a labor force for factories. And, inventors could **patent** (PAT-uhnt) what they made. The chance to earn a lot of money led many to try to create new inventions.

The British government had laws to support its businesses. When the British traded with its many colonies, it sought favorable terms for the merchants. Great Britain also had well-kept roads and canals. This made it easy to move and trade materials.

Laissez-Faire

In 1776, a new book recommended the idea of laissez-faire (leh-sa-FAIR). This means that the government should never interfere in business. There would be no laws to govern industry. Businesses would not need to show concerns for their workers.

Afraid of Machines

Until about 1850, mobs of people attacked and wrecked machines. They feared machines would someday take away their jobs. Before long, people saw that they could not avoid **technological** (tek-no-LOH-geh-cuhl) change.

America Joins the Revolution

The Industrial Revolution got a slow start in the New World. Some machines were in use by 1783. But it was not until after the Civil War that the real changes took place.

At first, American business owners found it hard to raise **capital**. Capital is money that can be borrowed. Instead, people wanted to invest in land because owning land was a sign of wealth.

Steam engines were first introduced during the Industrial Revolution. However, American manufacturers did not rush to use steam power. There were plenty of streams and rivers, so waterpower was favored. Also, the United States was a new nation. It had few roads, and they were muddy and had deep ruts. As a result, materials could not be moved easily.

American industry's growth was linked to the increased use of steel. Steel has more carbon than iron does. It is stronger and more flexible. It can be formed into almost anything. By 1860, it was used for machines, ships, bridges, and railroad tracks.

A Big Change

The United States went from depending on foreign goods in 1840 to producing nearly everything it needed by 1890. The value of goods created by American industry was 10 times greater in 1916 than in 1870!

No Riches for the South

The bulk of the industrial growth and wealth was in the North. This sparked resentment in the South. After losing the Civil War, the South saw the changes as another insult.

There were dirt roads like this one throughout the United States. That made it hard to move heavy machines and materials.

After the Civil War, big factories became a familiar sight in America.

Coal, Factories, and Cotton

American industry grew the fastest in Pennsylvania. This area had a ready supply of coal. Blast furnaces burn coal for fuel. They need fuel to turn iron ore into steel. These furnaces sprang up near the coal mines. Steel allowed railroads to spread across the nation. Railroads made it fast and easy to move items. Canals were dug so that boats could move goods, too.

Industrialists (in-DUHS-tree-uhl-istz) opened factories to make goods. Using machines, workers made products faster. The increased production made the nation's **economy** (ih-KAWN-uh-mee) grow. Businesses could charge less for their products. Then, more people could buy them. Sales were booming.

A girl uses a weaving machine in a cotton mill.

The **textile** (TEKS-tile), or cloth, industry was changed by machines. Before, people had spun thread, woven cloth, and made clothes by hand. They worked in their homes. Once machines were invented, these tasks moved into factories.

Since 1823, cotton had been Europe's favorite cloth. Even running at full speed, the textile mills could not keep up with the European demand.

I Think I Can!

In 1869, the United States completed the world's first transcontinental railroad system. It joined the East Coast to the West Coast. The distance of all rail lines in the United States grew to nearly 200,000 miles (322,000 km) by 1900!

A Terrible Side Effect

The growth of cotton cloth stimulated slavery. The nation went from 700,000 slaves in 1790 to four million in 1860. A majority of the slaves worked on cotton plantations.

Slaves pick cotton on a plantation in Mississippi.

King Car

Of all the innovations of the late 1800s, the car had the biggest impact on life. For most of history, the majority of people had lived and died within 25 miles of their birthplaces. Now, the car allowed people to go farther away from their homes.

Fast Assembly

In 1912, it took 12.5 worker hours to complete a Model T. The assembly line sped things up so much that just two years later, it took only 1.5 worker hours to make one car.

Henry Ford changed life in America.

Two men work the assembly line at a Ford car plant.

An Invention Convention

In the last part of the 1800s, people invented dozens of things. Some of these include the telegraph, the sewing machine, the typewriter, and the telephone. Also created at this time were the electric light bulb, the camera, and the gas engine. Never before had so many inventions been created in such a short period of time.

The gas engine led to a practical car. Although he was not the first to build a car, Henry Ford soon became the car-industry leader. He made the Model T in 1908, and more than 10,000 of them sold the first year.

The demand for cars was high, and Ford's company could not make them fast enough. So, Ford invented the **assembly line**. Men stood along a **conveyor belt** (kuhn-VAY-or belt). As each engine moved past, the worker did one job. One man placed a bolt. Another man put on the nut. A third man tightened it. The assembly line changed factory work forever.

These men are Western Union telegraph operators in New York City.

Take Me to the Bank!

Capital was very important to the rise of industry. Banks brought savers and industrialists together. People took their cash to banks. The banks gave them an **interest** rate of about one percent. This means people earned money by leaving their money in the banks. Then the banks lent out the money.

Bank loans were given to people who needed money to start or enlarge businesses. Over time, the people had to pay back the banks. The borrowers paid back the original amount plus three percent interest. Three percent is more than the one percent interest paid by banks. So, the banks made money because they got more money back than they paid in interest.

Another way to get capital was by issuing **stocks**. Stocks are part ownership in a company. A person gave the business owner cash. In return, he got a stock certificate. It stated that he owned a small part of the business. That meant that he would get a little bit of the profits. The more stock he held, the greater his ownership in the business.

Certificate of capital stock from 1876

The financial district of New York City in 1910

Bankers Produce

Bankers played a major role in developing large industries. By 1895, the United States was the largest, richest industrialized nation on Earth. It produced the majority of the world's steel, oil, wheat, and cotton.

The Risk of Banking

Bankers take a risk when they lend money. They will lose money If they lend funds to a business that fails or to a person who cannot pay it back.

J. P. Morgan, Financier

J. P. Morgan was a **financier** (fih-nan-SUHR), or banker. He got rich lending money to industrialists. He had a knack for knowing which businesses would grow. He made sure he lent money to them.

Thomas Edison, Inventor

Thomas Edison created the most inventions in American history. He held 1,093 U.S. patents! Not only was he an inventor, but he was also a businessman. He started the company General Electric (GE).

Carnegie educated himself by visiting a local library. To help educate others, he spent 55 million dollars to build over 2,500 libraries worldwide.

John D. Rockefeller was the first American billionaire.

Thomas Edison with the phonograph, one of his more popular inventions

Workers lay out plates of steel in a steel mill.

Wealthy Industrialists

An industrialist risks money on a business **venture** (VEN-chur) that he thinks will earn money. At the turn of the century, the risk paid off for quite a few men. They grew rich. Three of the best known are Andrew Carnegie (kar-NEH-gee), John D. Rockefeller, and Henry Ford.

Carnegie was a Scottish immigrant. At age 17, he started working for a railroad. There, he saw the importance of steel. He bought a steel mill and built it into the largest, most profitable one in America.

Oil has to be pulled up from the earth and refined. Then, it can be used to run machines and cars. Rockefeller made more than one billion dollars in the oil industry. He did this by buying out his competition. By 1879, he owned 90 percent of the U.S. oil industry. The fact that he owned so much made people upset.

Ford made the first car that the average worker could buy. He became a multimillionaire. The Ford Motor Company is still in business today.

It Stinks in the Sweatshops

Around 1800, United States factories were expanding. But there were no laws in place to **regulate** them. So, business owners often took advantage of their workers. They made them work for long hours and low wages. Even worse, they did not care if their workers faced hot, dirty, and dangerous conditions.

Some factory owners set up **sweatshops** in the cheapest places they could find. Often, these were dimly lit buildings with no windows. Sometimes people could not speak or use the bathroom! There was no such thing as a break. Many of the workers were women and children. They did not dare to argue about these conditions. They needed the cash. If they did not work, they had no money to buy food.

As early as 1830, people started to protest about the sweatshops. But the problem only got worse after 1880. That's when the number of immigrants coming to America increased. These immigrants needed jobs and were willing to work anywhere.

This group is working in a New York City sweatshop.

Newspapers across the country covered the Triangle Shirtwaist Company disaster.

The World.

154 KILLED IN SKYSCRAPER FACTORY FIRE; SCORES BURN, OTHERS LEAP TO DEATH.

700 WORKERS, MOSTLY GIRLS, TRAPPED; BODIES OF DEAD HEAP THE STREETS; ONLY ONE FIRE ESCAPE FOR ALL.

Employees Caught on Eighth, Ninth and Tenth Floors—The Blaze Spreads with Great Rapidity—Victims Jump from Window Ledges with Clothing Aflame and Pile Up Below, Dead and Dying—Life Nets Either Torn from Grasp of Rescuers or Burst by Force of Numbers—Criminal Negligence May Be Charged for Locked Fireproof Doors Leading to Stairs—Blaze Is in Triangle Waist Co. Rooms, Washington Place and Greene St.

A Terrible Fire

The Triangle Shirtwaist Company occupied the top three floors of a 10-story building in New York City. This tragedy made the government set up new laws about working conditions.

Work or Starve

Back then, if you wanted to eat, you had to work or beg. There were a few charities run by churches in big cities. But they were overrun by people needing food or somewhere to sleep. They had to turn away more people than they helped.

The Triangle Shirtwaist Company was one of these sweatshops. In 1911 a fire broke out. Bolts of fabric inside the wooden building provided fuel for the fire. The only fire escape collapsed when the women stepped on it. Exits were blocked or locked. With their hair and clothes on fire, women jumped to their deaths. A total of 154 people, most of them teenagers, died in the blaze.

Taking Advantage of Immigrant Labor

About 27 million immigrants came to America between 1880 and 1930. Most immigrants were from Europe. Some people came from China. Other immigrants came from Mexico and Canada. All of these people thought that they would have better lives in America. This was not always true.

Many immigrants arrived penniless. Yet they needed money to survive. They were easy **prey** for the sweatshop owners. The needlework and cigar-making industries used a lot of immigrant labor.

Many immigrants would work in any conditions for long hours and low pay. American workers felt that they would never get better conditions and wages. The constant flow of new people willing to put up with anything hurt working conditions.

Outside the sweatshops, entire immigrant families worked in their one-room apartments. They did **piecework** for pennies. Often their children did not get educations. They had no time.

Building a Railroad

To build the railroad across the nation, Chinese immigrants laid rails from west to east. Irish immigrants laid rails from east to west. They met at Promontory Point, Utah, on May 10, 1869.

Long Hours

In 1900, most laborers worked about 53 hours per week. Immigrants laborers usually worked at least 60–70 hours each week.

This family is working on piecework together.

Immigrants built the Transcontinental Railroad.

Immigrants came from all over the world.

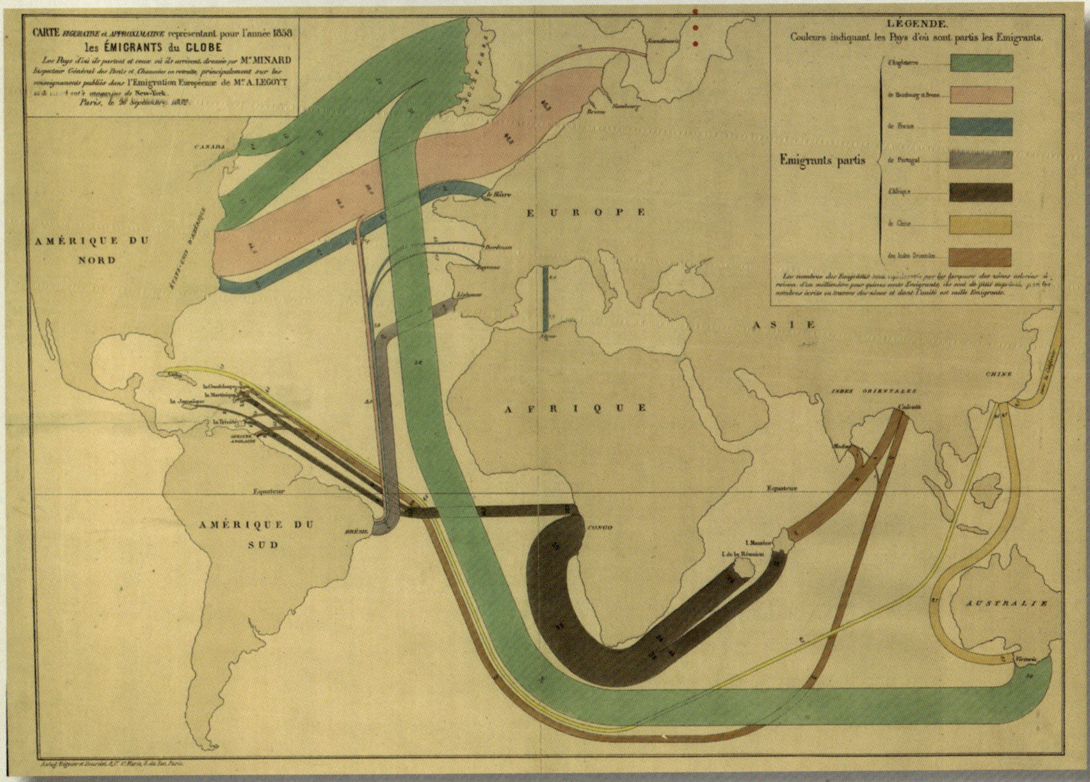

The Laboring Child

In the early 1900s, many children had to work instead of going to school. These children worked in such bad conditions that some of them were injured or killed. And since they had no time for school, they had no hope of escaping from the sweatshops, coal mines, and textile mills.

New England textile mill owners treated their workers badly. Knitting machines and fabric looms were dangerous. Children often worked on these machines. Children have small hands and fingers so they could fix the many parts of the machines. Lots of children who grew sleepy or could not move fast enough were hurt in these machines. The mill owners did not care. They knew there were other children to take the places of those who were injured or killed.

A photographer named Lewis Hine wanted to stop child labor. Around 1911, he took many photos of children working. He sent them to newspapers. His pictures showed children working in terrible conditions and awful places. Once people saw these photos, they began to press the government to end child labor.

Two young boys work the spinning machine in a cotton mill.

This poster encouraged people to stop child labor.

Startling Statistics

In 1832, almost half of the factory workers were between the ages of seven and sixteen. By 1860, only a handful of states had outlawed employment for children under the age of ten. Even in 1890, two out of every ten American children still worked six days a week.

The Orphan Trains

Many orphans lived on the streets of New York City. Children without jobs begged or stole food. In 1854, Charles Loring Brace decided to put these children on trains to the Midwest. He hoped farmers would adopt them. About 200,000 children were adopted this way.

President Theodore Roosevelt

Morgan's Monopoly

In 1904, President Theodore Roosevelt encouraged the U.S. Supreme Court to enforce the Sherman Antitrust Act against Morgan. His company was monopolizing the western railroads.

A Modern Monopoly

Microsoft® was convicted of having a monopoly. Its Windows® 95 operating system made people use Microsoft's Internet browser. The company had to pay damages. Its practices had hurt other software companies.

Trust Busting

There were some companies that wanted to control everything. So the Sherman Antitrust Act was passed in 1890. It was based on the government's right to regulate trade. The act's purpose was to stop big business from abusing its power.

First, the act banned **monopolies** (muh-NAWP-uh-leez). A monopoly is when one person or company has total control of a market or industry. Rich industrialists did not think that the United States government would enforce the law. Rockefeller tried to do business as usual. So did J. P. Morgan. But the U.S. Supreme Court made both men end their monopolies.

Second, the act stated that no company could form a **trust**. At that time, huge companies created trusts to control the market. First, the company bought most of its competitors. Then, it created trusts to force the rest of the competition to limit production and keep prices low. In effect, such a trust let one company "own" the whole industry.

The United States Supreme Court building is where the antitrust laws are enforced.

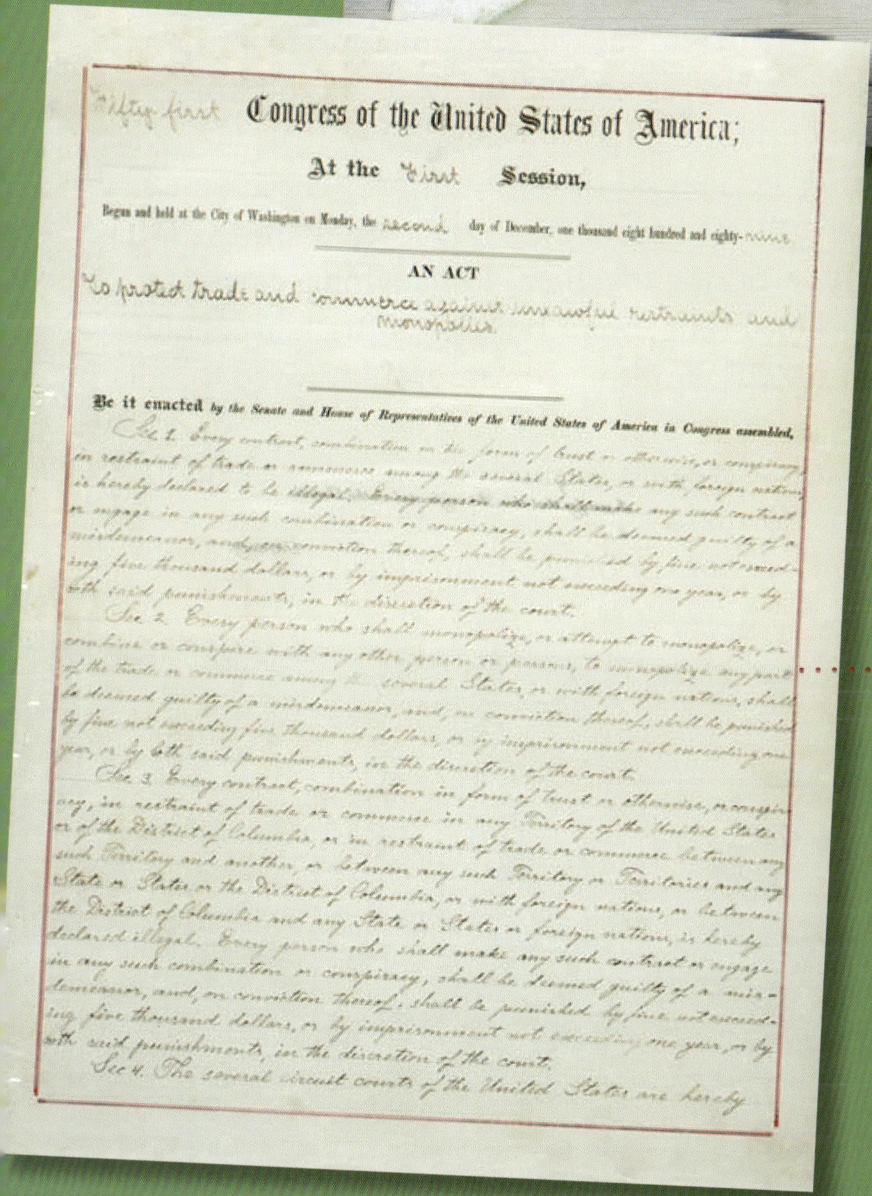

Fifty-first Congress of the United States of America;

At the First Session,

Begun and held at the City of Washington on Monday, the second day of December, one thousand eight hundred and eighty-nine.

AN ACT

To protect trade and commerce against unlawful restraints and monopolies.

Be it enacted by the Senate and House of Representatives of the United States of America in Congress assembled,

Sec. 1. Every contract, combination in the form of trust or otherwise, or conspiracy, in restraint of trade or commerce among the several States, or with foreign nations, is hereby declared to be illegal. Every person who shall make any such contract or engage in any such combination or conspiracy, shall be deemed guilty of a misdemeanor, and, on conviction thereof, shall be punished by fine not exceeding five thousand dollars, or by imprisonment not exceeding one year, or by both said punishments, in the discretion of the court.

Sec. 2. Every person who shall monopolize, or attempt to monopolize, or combine or conspire with any other person or persons, to monopolize any part of the trade or commerce among the several States, or with foreign nations, shall be deemed guilty of a misdemeanor, and, on conviction thereof, shall be punished by fine not exceeding five thousand dollars, or by imprisonment not exceeding one year, or by both said punishments, in the discretion of the court.

Sec. 3. Every contract, combination in form of trust or otherwise, or conspiracy, in restraint of trade or commerce in any Territory of the United States or of the District of Columbia, or in restraint of trade or commerce between any such Territory and another, or between any such Territory or Territories and any State or States or the District of Columbia, or with foreign nations, or between the District of Columbia and any State or States or foreign nations, is hereby declared illegal. Every person who shall make any such contract or engage in any such combination or conspiracy, shall be deemed guilty of a misdemeanor, and, on conviction thereof, shall be punished by fine not exceeding five thousand dollars, or by imprisonment not exceeding one year, or by both said punishments, in the discretion of the court.

Sec. 4. The several circuit courts of the United States are hereby

The Sherman Antitrust Act stopped businesses from abusing their power.

Labor Unions Get Their Start

Only business owners could afford the machines used to make goods. This gave them the upper hand. They showed no concern for their workers.

The workers realized that they must join together. So they formed labor unions. A labor union is a group of workers who agree to work together. They defend their rights at work. Sometimes, they have to go on strike to make sure they are treated fairly. If all the workers go on strike, a factory will grind to a halt.

Printers and shoemakers started the first unions. These were local groups. They never lasted more than a few years. In 1827, the different unions started working together. Philadelphia carpenters wanted a 10-hour workday. They went on strike. Bricklayers and printers did, too. It worked! Working conditions improved for all three groups.

Soon other groups did the same. Unions managed to get a 10-hour workday to be standard by the 1850s. But then, the unions got bogged down trying to bring about social reforms.

Western Union employees strike against low wages.

Actors go on strike in New York City in 1919.

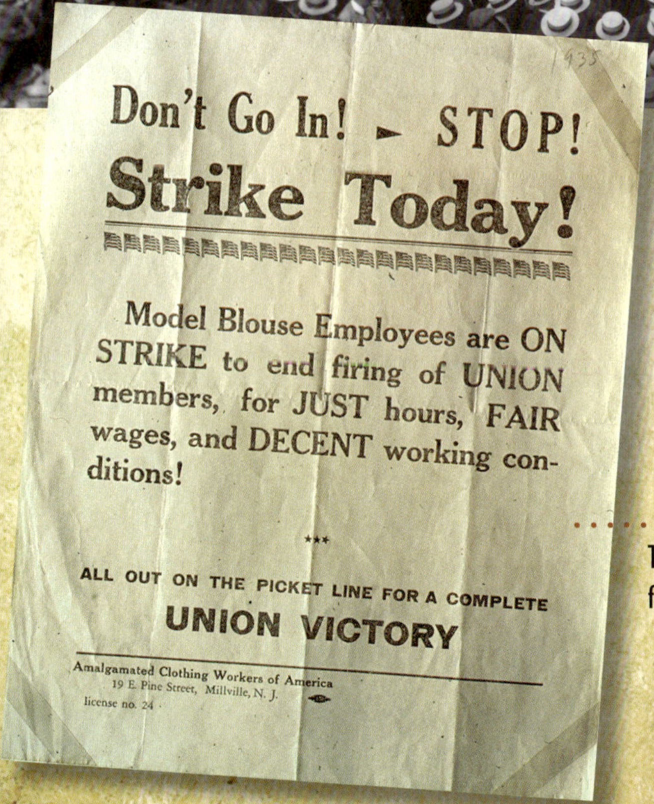
Don't Go In! ► STOP!

Strike Today!

Model Blouse Employees are ON STRIKE to end firing of UNION members, for JUST hours, FAIR wages, and DECENT working conditions!

***

ALL OUT ON THE PICKET LINE FOR A COMPLETE

UNION VICTORY

Amalgamated Clothing Workers of America
19 E. Pine Street, Millville, N. J.
license no. 24

This is a strike flyer from 1935.

The AFL

The American Federation of Labor (AFL) was the first successful union because it concentrated on workers' issues instead of social issues. The AFL leader asked owners to increase wages and to hold a person's job for him while he was out sick.

Employers Fight Back

Not surprisingly, employers did not like the unions. If a union leader called for a strike, the employer took him to court. There, the union leader was found to be violating the Sherman Antitrust Act. His actions were interfering with business. Judges demanded that strikes be ended.

Troubled Times for Unions

The Story Behind the Haymarket Riot

Workers in Chicago had gone on strike. The strikers threatened anyone who crossed the picket lines. One day, the police fired into the crowd of unarmed strikers. Many strikers were wounded and four died. The next day turned even more violent with the bomb attack.

The Pullman Strike of 1894

Workers at the Pullman Palace Car Company went on strike. The owners had cut their pay. The Railway Union tried to help by going on strike, too. But the U.S. government sent troops to end the strike. The strikes had interfered with the delivery of mail by train.

A number of conflicts occurred that nearly ended labor unions. The first happened in 1886. It is called the Haymarket Riot. Workers gathered in Chicago. They wanted to prevent the police from stopping a factory strike. Someone threw a bomb. Seven policemen and another person died. As a result, some of the union leaders were executed.

The Homestead Strike of 1892 was another setback. Steel workers went on strike for better pay. The owner hired guards to walk new workers into the plant. Fighting broke out and some people died. The workers quit the union and went back to work.

Unions got a big boost with the Immigration Act of 1924. It cut the number of people allowed into the United States each year. This limited the number of job seekers. So, this raised the workers' bargaining power. When the National Labor Relations Act passed in 1935, it forced employers to start bargaining with unions.

The scene at Haymarket Square on the night of May 4, 1886

FRANK LESLIE'S ILLUSTRATED WEEKLY

HOMESTEAD TROUBLES.

NEW YORK, JULY 14, 1892.

[PRICE, 10 CENTS.

THE LABOR TROUBLES AT HOMESTEAD, PENNSYLVANIA—ATTACK OF THE STRIKERS AND THEIR SYMPATHIZERS ON THE SURRENDERED PINKERTON MEN.—DRAWN BY MISS G. A. DAVIS, FROM A SKETCH BY C. UPHAM.—[SEE PAGE 43.]

The Homestead Strike was headline news in 1892.

The first troops arrive in Homestead on July 12, 1892.

Muckrakers Target Big Businesses

Have you ever heard the saying, "The pen is mightier than the sword"? This means that written words are more powerful than any weapon. **Muckrakers** were people who used their pens against big business. Muckrakers investigated businesses. Then, they wrote articles and books about the businesses. They described a lot of shocking things. This caused public scandals and, in some cases, government involvement.

A famous muckraker was Upton Sinclair. He wrote *The Jungle*. He described meat-packing plants. There, people prepared cows and pigs for food. The work took place in filthy conditions. In Sinclair's book, one man had his finger destroyed by the grinder. His flesh went into sausage. It was packaged and sent out to the public to eat! This book was very upsetting to the public. It led to the Pure Food and Drug Act of 1906.

Muckrakers got people to think about working conditions and how people ought to be treated. As a result, labor unions grew stronger. New laws were passed to help improve working conditions.

Today, there are better working conditions for people. Laws protect workers from bad situations. Laws keep children and others from sweatshops. And business owners cannot monopolize the industry. These changes are due to unions, laws, and muckrakers who made workplaces both safe and fair.

Conditions do not look very clean at this meat-packing plant in Chicago.

King Coal

Sinclair also wrote *King Coal* in 1917. This book exposed the awful working conditions of Colorado coal miners. He wanted to show that they had good reasons to strike. Later, he wrote *Oil!* This work helped to support the demands of labor unions.

A Famous Female Muckraker

Ida Tarbell was one of the first muckrakers. She wrote *The History of the Standard Oil Company* in 1901. In it, she told how John D. Rockefeller had used illegal practices to get control of the oil industry. This helped the U.S. Supreme Court to uphold the Sherman Antitrust Act.

Social activist and author Upton Sinclair made a difference.

Ida Tarbell

Glossary

assembly line—an arrangement of workers where an item moves along a conveyer belt and workers add to the item as it moves along until the whole piece is assembled

capital—money; often used to start a business

conveyor belt—a continuously moving band that transports things from one point to another

economy—the way a nation runs its industry, trade, and finance

financier—a person who lends funds to organizations to make money

industrialists—people who own or control manufacturing businesses

interest—a fee paid for borrowing money

monopolies—total control of markets or industries

muckrakers—people who write about corruption in society to try to change laws

patent—a legal document giving the inventor of an item the sole right to manufacture or sell it

piecework—work where wages are earned based on the number of pieces sewed

prey—victims

regulate—to bring under control of the law

revolution—to cause change or reform in the way things are done

stocks—shares in a company that show ownership and a right to receive part of the profits

sweatshops—businesses with poor working conditions; workers were often children and women

technological—having to do with technology or machines

textile—a woven or knit cloth

trust—an arrangement in which a person (trustee) holds or uses property for the benefit of others

venture—a business idea or project

Index

Image Credits

cover The Granger Collection, New York; p.1 The Granger Collection, New York; p.4 The Granger Collection, New York; p.5 Photos.com; p.7 (top) Roman Naumov/iStockphoto.com; p.7 (bottom) MPI/Getty Images; p.8 The Library of Congress; pp.8–9 The Library of Congress; p.10 (top) The Library of Congress; p.10 (bottom) Bettmann/Corbis; pp.10–11 North Wind Picture Archives/Alamy; p.12 The Library of Congress; p.13 The Library of Congress; p.14 (top) The Library of Congress; p.14 (middle) The Library of Congress; p.14 (bottom) The Library of Congress; p.15 The Library of Congress; p.16 The Library of Congress; p.17 The Library of Congress; p.18 The Library of Congress; p.19 (top) The Granger Collection, New York; p.19 (bottom) The Library of Congress; p.20 The National Archives; p.21 Bass Museum of Art/Corbis; p.22 The Library of Congress; p.23 (top) Jonathan Larsen/Shutterstock, Inc.; p.23 (bottom) The National Archives; p.24 Bettmann/Corbis; p.25 (top) The Library of Congress; p.25 (bottom) The Granger Collection, New York; p.27 (top left) Library of Congress; p.27 (top right) Library of Congress; p.27 (bottom) Library of Congress; p.28 The Library of Congress; pp.28–29 The Granger Collection, New York; p.29 (left) The Library of Congress; p.29 (right) The Library of Congress